Reviews

"Delicious, simple recipes . . .
Comfort food, at its best."
—Fire Up The Oven Blog

"Ava makes reading these recipes fun with her
personal interjections and humor. But for a cook,
this is like a treasured gold mine volume of down
home comfort foods."
—Fab Fantasy Fiction

"Full of wonderful, mouthwatering recipes,
Ms. Miles puts another piece of herself into this
collection . . ."
—Tome Tender

"Ms. Miles draws from her experience as an
apprentice chef . . . and it shows . . . I loved {the}
authenticity of the food references, and the
recipes . . . looked divine."
—BlogCritics

Home Baked Happiness

Recipes and Reflections on Home and Happiness

BY

Ava Miles

To all of the readers who begged me for a baking cookbook. Thank you for treasuring my stories and our mutual love of food. You are my home baked happiness in more ways than you can know.

To my family and all of the happy meals ahead...

And to French Chef and my divine entourage for continuing to show me home baked happiness starts inside and is a miracle to be shared with ourselves and others.

Contents

I often remember my grandmother when I'm cooking since she taught me. But it's more than that. Cooking with her was usually loving and happy. From the time I could help her, I felt the love gracing her kitchen. Her recipe box was packed with special treats written from women in the family who had passed away but whose memory she still kept alive. She'd tell me stories about my great-grandmother, who had "the touch" and could always make mouth-watering—and filling—meals for her family of twelve.

I loved to see all of these women's handwriting on the recipe cards we'd pull out for a meal. Recipes take on a new meaning when they're passed down this way. We remember the deceased loved one who gave us this recipe. We smile when we share it with other people. We get to share a story about, say, our grandma, who used to make this cake or that cookie every Christmas Eve or that birthday.

Cooking connects us to love.

And home.

~ Excerpt from Ava's Goddesses Eat

Growing up, baking was part of home. I didn't realize how special it was until my friends came over to play and would gasp with giddiness at the awesome bucket of cookies, the piping hot cinnamon rolls, and the golden-crusted pies at our house.

Of course now I know baking was the way the women in my family created a home. Baking was a way of showing love. Baked good were bite-sized happiness.

When I set off into the world on my own, I'd make family recipes when I was homesick. When my grandma passed away, I'd bake the recipes she'd taught me. Those happy times would filter through my memory as I sat down and enjoyed the delicious treat I'd made.

Now I have a home of my own...and since baking makes me so happy, it makes others happy too. It's not just the mouthwatering treats. It's the jovial atmosphere in the kitchen. It's the connection as we dance and cook together.

It's the home baked happiness.

Ava

Savory Breads

*O*nce everyone had a glass, Andre raised his to her. "To Margie from America. May she learn to bake bread like a Frenchman."

"French woman, ma cherie," Belle said, nudging him in the ribs.

"As you wish," he said with a laugh. "To making the bread of life."

The words held a spiritual significance she'd never fully understood before. Bread was life. She'd known that for some time. Now she understood the deeper nuances of that statement. Bread did give life. It had given her life. And now she wanted to share that life with others—like she had with Evan. Her new knowledge humbled her mightily.

"To making the bread of life," she said and connected their glasses in the toast.

~ Excerpt from Ava's
Dare Valley Meets Paris Billionaire

$\mathcal{S}$ome might assert that fire was the first magical creation on earth, but I'd say bread was a close second...

Nothing feels like home more than bread. My fascination and love for bread baking started young. I was raised by women who made bread for their family and friends, and it was something I wanted to learn and share with those I loved. There's a special magic to making bread rise, of filling it with delicious ingredients and wrapping it up tight. Piping hot it comes out of the oven to tempt. Steam swirls up like mist from its luscious texture. With every bite, I always feel transformed. The sensory experience nourishes my very soul and reminds me of home. And it makes me happy.

I've studied at my grandmother's side and with a leading baker in Paris, the city where bread fills the imagination everywhere through sparkling store-front windows. As my own woman now, I make breads from the past and ones new to me as a way of sharing love and experiencing the magic made by mixing yeast, water, and four, and other ingredients. Bread can be so simple. It can be so involved. Regardless, the result is always the same: magnificent.

AVA'S FRENCH BREAD

If there is one thing I fully understand about French bread after studying with a baker, it's that every person's French bread is a particular to them. Perhaps more than any other bread, this one seems to radiate the contents of your soul. These days, I make a huge batch of French bread, shape the loaves, and freeze whatever I'm not going to bake that day. This recipe is perfect for that. And it makes it all the easier when you want to have fresh bread, but don't feel like making it.

Allow yourself to expand as a bread maker with this recipe. In the beginning, when the yeast and I were still becoming friends, my bread didn't seem to rise as high as those in a French bakery. But I stuck with it. I listened to the dough with my hands and my heart. I experimented with different cooking techniques. I finally settled on baking the bread on a pizza stone. Now, when you cut into one of my loaves, it's crusty on the outside and light and airy on the inside. That accomplishment makes me happy. After all, what signifies home-baked happiness better than French bread?

> 2 tablespoons yeast
> 1½ tablespoons salt
> 3½ cups warm water
> 6 cups flour

Measure out the yeast and the salt and then add the water. Stir until everything has incorporated. Let proof for 10-15 minutes until the mixture is bubbly on the top. Add the flour, mixing thoroughly. Let rise for one hour until the bread has doubled in size. Turn onto a floured surface and knead a little more until the bread is smooth in texture and not sticky. At this point, you may have bubbles in your dough. That's a good thing!

Shape into loaves. Again, use your imagination. You can make a classic loaf shape or a circle (by pinching the ends together). The baker I trained with even braids the bread like you would hair, and it comes out beautifully. I only do this when I'm feeling inspired. I typically use a razor blade to cut the diagonal slices in the top of the bread. I've found that even my sharp knives don't deliver the kind of cut I want. Experiment with what works for you. Most of all have fun!

FOCACCIA BREAD

Few breads are as tantalizing as focaccia, especially when the rosemary is picked straight from your own garden. Serve this with a summer salad or a side of pasta and let the aromatic bread lighten your heart.

Bread

2½ teaspoons yeast

1⅓ cups warm water

⅓ cup olive oil

2 teaspoons salt

3 cups flour

Mix the top four ingredients until the yeast is dissolved. Let the mixture proof for 15 minutes until the yeast bubbles on top. Then mix the flour into the bread. Let rise for one hour. Then roll out onto a floured surface and form the dough into a round disc.

Topping

Touch of olive oil

2 tablespoons rosemary

2 teaspoons coarse salt

Once you have shaped the bread to your satisfaction, brush the dough with olive oil and shake the rosemary and salt on top. Let rise for another 30-40 minutes. Bake at 425 degrees for 15-20 minutes until golden brown.

IRISH SODA BREAD

Even though there's a lot of Irish in my family, I didn't grow up with this bread. I first discovered it in Irish bars when I lived in the Washington DC area, listening to Irish bands and watching Notre Dame football with other alums. The bread was good, but it was only when I visited Ireland that I came home with the urge to make this bread. It seemed perfect for cold nights when I made soup or stew.

After much experimenting, I finally discovered the secret. Buttermilk! Otherwise, the bread was too dry. This bread is a family favorite, and I like to think about my ancestors as I make it, living in thatched cottages on that magical island we call Ireland before they made the trip to America with the hope of a better life.

4 tablespoons butter

1¾ cups flour

1¾ cups wheat flour

1 teaspoon baking soda

½ teaspoon salt

2½ cups buttermilk

1 tablespoon dark brown sugar

3 tablespoons oat bran

3 tablespoons wheat germ

3 tablespoons old-fashioned oats (or spelt)

Thoroughly grease or butter a loaf pan. Set aside. Cut the butter into the dry ingredients of white and wheat flour, soda, and salt until the mixture is crumbly. Mix in the buttermilk with the brown sugar and then add in the oat bran, wheat germ, and oats. Stir until completely incorporated. Pour the bread into the loaf pan; it will be sticky. Bake at 425 degrees for about 35-40 minutes until you can insert a toothpick and have it come out clean. When the bread is finished, let rest in the pan for 5-10 minutes and then using a knife, make sure the sides aren't stuck, and turn the bread out onto a cooling rack. Enjoy with butter or jam or simply plain.

JISKIES

Having trouble pronouncing this one? Well, I'm not even completely sure how to spell it honestly, but it's pronounced JIS-KEYS. Growing up, my grandma and mom would make these intoxicating cheese-filled treats when they were baking bread for cinnamon rolls and kolaches and the like. The problem is you don't want to eat just one.

When I tried to find the history on it, all I could postulate was that someone in the family must have made up this recipe. I have no idea who, but I have a feeling it was my great-grandmother, who was a legendary cook in the family. She had ten children, and I remember my grandma telling me that she could stretch food for the whole family and still make it taste delicious and be filling. They were hit hard by the Depression like most folks. Many of her recipes are with simple ingredients, and this one is no different.

I'm including it because it was one of my favorite breads growing up, but also because it's the epitome of home-baked happiness. What is it, you might ask? It's individual bread nuggets filled with cheddar cheese that's fried to perfection. Other people—not me—sprinkled the bread with powdered sugar. Regardless of its origin, this bread recipe is special and one I plan to share with the generations who come after me.

Dough

　　1 cup milk
　　¼ cup sugar

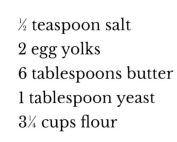

½ teaspoon salt

2 egg yolks

6 tablespoons butter

1 tablespoon yeast

3¼ cups flour

Filling

3 inch sticks of cheddar cheese, as much as needed

Warm the milk with the sugar and salt in the microwave or on the stove. Proof the yeast with 2 tablespoons of the mixture. When it is bubbly, add the rest of the milk mixture and eggs yolks, mixing quickly. Melt the butter. Add in the flour and butter and mix until the dough is sticky and yet supple. Let rise for one hour.

Roll the dough out onto a floured surface and knead it for a minute into a ball shape. Now cut off a piece of dough and roll it out until it's about three inches long and two inches wide. Again, play with the dimensions. It's not like I bring out a ruler when I bake. Take one cheddar cheese stick and place it in the middle of the dough piece. You can obviously cut your own sticks from a block of cheddar or buy them in stick form in the supermarket. Wrap the dough around the cheddar and seal the edges. Repeat the process of cutting the dough, wrapping up the cheese, and sealing the edges until you have run out of dough or made as many as you wish.

Now, heat some vegetable or canola oil in a pan.

The awesome thing about jiskies is that you can fry them in a little oil or deep-fry them. Your choice. Either way, you're going to want to turn them when the sides become golden brown. Lay them onto a plate lined with a paper towel, give them a minute or so to cool, and then start eating. Once you've tasted these treats, you're going to carve out time to make them again and again.

Sweet Breads

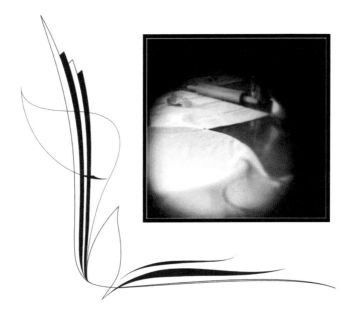

"When I tasted their cinnamon rolls for the first time, something happened to me."

She'd just moved to Dare Valley and was on her way to Don't Soy With Me for the late shift. Someone came out of Kemstead's bakery, and she caught a whiff of cinnamon and baking bread. She decided to treat herself to a cinnamon roll for braving the horrible weather when all she wanted was to call in sick and snuggle up on the couch in her fleece PJs and watch chick flicks.

Time stood still when she took that first bite. Her eyes fluttered shut. Her nose was saturated with the smells of cinnamon and caramel and a part of her soul cried out, Yes, this is what you've been looking for.

Her mother had never cooked. They'd hired a string of high-priced private chefs, and while the food had always been excellent, something had been missing.... In that one cinnamon roll, she'd found it. The mingled flavors of comfort, love, and the sweetness of life were rolled up in the bread's very layers. Her heart burst open. She got teary-eyed—not her usual—and she fell in love. With the taste as much as the sensation.

From that moment onward, she'd been eager to share that wonderful feeling with others.

~ Excerpt from Ava's
Dare Valley Meets Paris Billionaire

It all started with our family cinnamon rolls...

Somewhere back in the generations, someone decided to roll out our family sweet dough recipe and layer it with cinnamon, sugar, and melted butter and then roll it back up again and cut it into fat haystack-shaped buns. But that wasn't enough. No, cream and sugar and even more melted butter was mixed and poured over the top, resulting in the most decadent caramelized topping.

Our family was known for them. We all waited around the kitchen whenever a batch was in the oven. We protested when cinnamon rolls left the house for church bake sales or holiday presents. You better believe this was one recipe I was going to master.

And yet I discovered there were other sweet breads, ones not governed by yeast. They could include chocolate—always on my mind—or pumpkin. I found myself falling in love with these delightfully sweet treats and sharing them with those I love.

CINNAMON ROLLS

These cinnamon rolls are so magical I created a special bakery in my fictional Dare Valley series that made them. Through my beloved heroine, Margie Lancaster, these rolls have captured the imagination of many readers. I was unable to share this recipe when those books came out due to the death of my best friend and neighbor, Julia.

Now I'm happy to include this spectacular recipe for you and your loved ones to try. And trust me, it takes some practice, but well worth the effort. When I make them, I don't just think about all of the women in my family who have made them generation after generation. I think about that special town I've created that millions of readers have come to love as much as I do. Now that's what I call home baked happiness...

Dough

    1 cup milk

    ¼ cup sugar

    ½ teaspoon salt

    2 egg yolks

    6 tablespoons butter

    1 tablespoon yeast

    3¼ cups flour

Filling

> ½ cup sugar
>
> 1 tablespoon cinnamon
>
> 3 tablespoons butter

Topping

> ¾ cup whipping cream
>
> ¼ cup sugar
>
> 1 tablespoon cinnamon
>
> 3 tablespoons butter

Warm the milk with the sugar and salt in the microwave or on the stove. Proof the yeast with 2 tablespoons of the mixture. When it is bubbly, add the rest of the milk mixture and eggs yolks, mixing quickly. Melt the butter. Add in the flour and butter and mix until the dough is sticky and yet supple. Let rise for one hour.

Roll the dough out onto a floured surface and knead it for a minute into a ball shape. Using the rolling pin, roll the dough out until it is about a half an inch thick in a rectangle. Spread the melted butter on top to thinly cover it and then sprinkle the cinnamon and sugar evenly over the dough.

Roll up into a loaf. The butter sometimes oozes out, so don't worry. Cut the bread into rolls about three inches high and place in a greased baking pan. You're going to arrange them a few inches apart with the layered circle of the roll showing. Let rise for another 15-20 minutes and then bake

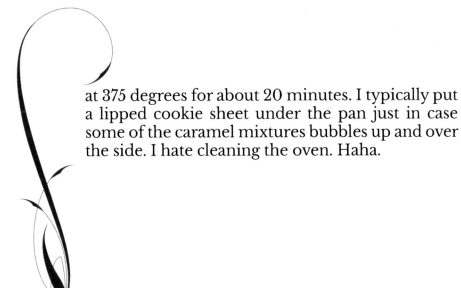

at 375 degrees for about 20 minutes. I typically put a lipped cookie sheet under the pan just in case some of the caramel mixtures bubbles up and over the side. I hate cleaning the oven. Haha.

KOLACHES

These magical Czech bite-sized breads were always around on special holidays growing up. Again, I have no idea who started making them. It might have been my great-grandmother. All I know is that they are freaking delicious. And you can use the same dough we used for the cinnamon rolls. It's the basic sweet dough recipe honestly.

While I grew up with my grandma making poppy seed kolaches, those aren't my favorite. Thank goodness, she and my mom made apricot and cherry ones as well. We used to cluster around the kitchen when these would come out of the oven. I remember learning how to make them when I was a young girl. It takes some getting used to, but I know you can make them too if you want. They are well worth the effort.

Dough

> 1 cup milk
>
> ¼ cup sugar
>
> ½ teaspoon salt
>
> 2 egg yolks
>
> 6 tablespoons butter
>
> 1 tablespoon yeast
>
> 3¼ cups flour

Warm the milk with the sugar and salt in the microwave or on the stove. Proof the yeast with

2 tablespoons of the mixture. When it is bubbly, add the rest of the milk mixture and eggs yolks, mixing quickly. Melt the butter. Add in the flour and butter and mix until the dough is sticky and yet supple. Let rise for one hour.

When the dough is ready, you're going to want to roll it onto a floured surface and make buns. How do you do this? Cut a piece of dough and shape it into a flat ball. Here's where you have to play with technique. I was taught to tuck the ball of dough in my palm until it became the desired shape.

Place the rolls on a greased baking sheet. Brush them with butter. Let them rise for one hour. While they are rising, you're going to prepare your filling. This isn't difficult. You're going to choose what sounds good to you. If you want cherry kolaches, simply use cherry pie filling. If you want apricot, simply cut up some dried apricots, add some water, and cook on the stove until they are a smooth paste. Some people have used applesauce I understand, but never in our family. Doesn't mean that wouldn't be good. Use your imagination. Again, this kind of bread is a *vehicle* for flavor.

When the rolls have risen, insert your index fingers and pull in opposite directions to create a hole in the middle. Be sure not to puncture the bottom of the roll though, but if you do, no big deal. It's just baking. Add your magical filling to the hole in the bread, being sure not to overflow it. Bake the kolaches at 400 degrees for 8-10 minutes, transferring from the bottom to the top shelf while baking.

After taking them out of the oven, allow them to cool just a touch. I've burned the roof of my mouth more than once being impetuous and eating them too quickly out of the oven. That's how delicious they are.

PUMPKIN CHOCOLATE BREAD

This bread always starts calling to me with the first brush of fall, as the leaves turn gold and crimson and the nights start to cool. I've done a lot of experimenting with this bread to make it lighter, and the trick is to beat the egg whites and fold them into the batter. I've also started to use honey instead of sugar since I adore it, and all you need to do is add a little more soda.

2 cups flour

1 teaspoon baking soda (1½ teaspoons soda if use honey)

2 teaspoons baking powder

½ teaspoon of salt

½ cup butter

¾ cup sugar (or ¼ cup honey)

3 eggs

1 cup mashed pumpkin

½ teaspoon grated ginger

1 teaspoon cinnamon

½ teaspoon nutmeg

¼ teaspoon cloves

1 cup chocolate chips

¾ cup nuts

Melt the butter. Mix in the pumpkin, butter, and sugar/honey. Beat the egg yolks and stir thoroughly. Add dry ingredients and stir well.

Mix in the chocolate chips and nuts. Beat the egg whites and then gently fold them into the batter.

Pour into a greased/buttered loaf pan. Bake at 350 degrees for 45 minutes. Reduce heat to 325 and bake another 15 minutes until the toothpick you insert comes out clean. Rest in the loaf pan for 15 minutes before turning it out onto a baking rack to cool.

CHOCOLATE BUNS

While I've trained in Paris to make croissants (mostly because I love the chocolate ones so much), I've found it challenging to make them on my own so far. In the absence of mastery, I love making chocolate buns instead. They give me the same happy feeling with a lot less work and fuss, and that's something this goddess woman appreciates.

Dough

> ¾ cup milk
>
> 1½ tablespoons sugar
>
> ⅓ teaspoon salt
>
> 1 teaspoon vanilla
>
> 2 teaspoons yeast
>
> 3 tablespoons butter
>
> 2 eggs
>
> 3 cups flour

Filling

Semi-sweet milk chocolate chips, as needed

Warm the milk and add the sugar, salt, and vanilla, stirring until everything has dissolved. Add 2 tablespoons of the milk mixture to the yeast and proof until bubbly. Beat the eggs. Melt the butter. Add the flour to the yeast along with the milk and then the eggs and butter. Stir until incorporated. Let rise for one hour.

Roll the dough into large rectangle about one-fourth an inch thick. Cut the dough into squares, large enough to fold into the bun size of your choice. Place 1 tablespoon chocolate chips onto each square and fold the dough so the chocolate is encased in the dough. Make sure to pinch the ends to seal the filling. Place the dough onto buttered baking sheets. Bake at 350 degrees for 20-25 minutes.

BANANA CHOCOLATE BREAD

If there's one thing I adore it's chocolate, as you've probably guessed. Anywhere I can add chocolate without overpowering a classic recipe, I will. Hence adding chocolate chips to our family banana bread recipe. I love the creaminess of the melted chocolate in the bread. Again, another simple favorite that feels like home.

    1 cup mashed bananas

    1 tablespoon lemon juice

    ¾ cup sugar

    8 tablespoons butter

    2 eggs

    2 cups flour

    1 teaspoon baking soda

    2 teaspoons baking powder

    ½ teaspoon salt

    1 cup chocolate chips

    1 cup ground walnuts

Mash the bananas and lemon juice and set aside. Grind the nuts and set aside as well. Cream together the sugar and butter. Add the eggs and mix until incorporated. I like to add the mashed banana mixture at this point and stir.

Now it's time to add the dry ingredients, starting with the flour and then the soda, baking powder, and salt; I prefer to add them in this order to prevent the rising agents from activating too early. Mix these ingredients together and then fold in the chocolate chips and ground walnuts as well. Spread the mixture evenly in a buttered loaf pan. Bake at 350 for 55-60 minutes.

CHERRY PIE BARS

Growing up, these bars were special treats when we'd come home from school. I remember doing my homework while I ate one, trying not to get the crumbs or cherry filling on my papers. They run a little more sweet than my usual, but the sheer hominess of them made these bars a must addition for home baked happiness.

Bars

1½ cups sugar

16 tablespoons butter

4 eggs

3 cups flour

2½ tablespoons baking powder

½ teaspoon salt

1 teaspoon vanilla

1 can cherry pie filling

Cream the sugar and butter. Add the eggs and blend together. Add the dry ingredients of flour, salt, and baking powder and mix. Spread two-thirds of the mixture on a greased jelly roll pan and then make a layer with the cherry pie filling. Drop the remaining batter over the cherry layer with a teaspoon to create a dotted effect. Bake at 350 degrees for 35 minutes.

Icing

    1 cup powdered sugar

    1 teaspoon vanilla

    water

Add enough water to the powdered sugar and vanilla to drizzle over the cooled bars. FYI: the icing will melt if the bars are still hot. I've made that mistake before. Haha.

Biscuits

"When my grandma passed, there was this huge hole inside me. She taught me how to cook, and she said that those of us who love to feed people are obsessed with finding the perfect ingredient—the one thing that fills the emptiness inside us with peace.

"My grandma's perfect ingredient was having a glass of honey water and sitting on the back porch steps. Mine is the chipotle hot sauce from New Orleans that I add to the butter I use on my sourdough bread every morning as I watch the sun rise. Terrance, you need to search for your own perfect ingredient. Once you find it, you'll have peace..."

~ Excerpt from Ava's The Perfect Ingredient

My love affair with biscuits started with the buttermilk variety. Being from the Midwest, we were a meat-and-potatoes kind of family, and more often than not, my mom or grandma would make biscuits to accompany a beef or pork roast we were having for dinner. There was one particular large frosted glass my mom would stand on her tippy toes to bring down and use to cut the biscuits into large circles. Now that I think about it, this is where I first encountered that magical elixir called buttermilk. In my opinion, it transforms everything it touches; making bread rise, making it moist, making it magical.

I've since expanded into other biscuits. When I moved to the South for a long spell, I discovered what perfect companions they are to my fried chicken, BBQ, and other delights. My repertoire with biscuits continued to expand as I tried new flavors and ingredients.

Because nothing says home baked happiness like a hot buttered biscuit...

HEAVENLY BUTTERMILK BISCUITS

This recipe has been featured before in my Country Heaven Cookbook, but it's so darn good I had to share it again in case you missed it. I'm a biscuit lover to the core because of this recipe; they were my first. These biscuits are simply heaven in bread form.

6 tablespoons butter

2 cups flour

1 tablespoon sugar

¼ teaspoon baking soda

2½ teaspoons baking powder

½ teaspoon salt

¾ cup buttermilk

Cut the butter into the dry ingredients until the mixture is crumbly. Then add the buttermilk and stir until incorporated, but try not to over mix. On a floured surface, pat the dough out until it is an inch thickness and then cut into circles with a glass (flour the rim). Feel free to use the scraps to make another biscuit; sometimes I make it into a special shape like a heart since the dough is less uniform. Then I give that one to someone special, especially if they've had a tough day. Place on a greased cookie sheet and bake at 450 degrees for 12-15 minutes.

CHEESE BISCUITS

Cheese is my savory go-to like chocolate is my sweet lover. Since jalapeno cheese cornbread is one of my favorites, I had to have a cheese biscuit. This recipe doesn't disappoint. In fact, a dear friend from Memphis said they were the best biscuits he'd ever had; and people from that city know food.

4 tablespoons butter

1½ cups flour

1½ teaspoons baking powder

½ teaspoon salt

2 eggs

¾ cup milk

¼ teaspoon vanilla

⅓ cup sugar

1 cup shredded cheese

Cut the butter into the flour, salt, and baking powder until the mixture is crumbly. Beat the eggs. Then add in the eggs, milk, vanilla, and sugar and stir in the sugar until incorporated. Fold in the shredded cheese (I love cheddar, but you can experiment with your favorite). Roll the dough out to about one inch thickness and cut either into circles or squares (biscuits are traditionally round, but who says we can't break a few rules?). Lay them out a few inches apart on a greased cookie sheet. Bake at 400 degrees for 15-20 minutes.

PARMESAN PECAN BISCUITS

If the head chef I worked with ever knew I've added parmesan to my biscuits, he'd probably kill me. I'm half joking. When I worked in a Northern Italian restaurant a long while back, I discovered the full power of fresh parmesan. I grew up with what I'll sweetly refer to as parmesan "dust." We covered our spaghetti and pizza with it growing up. I didn't know that parmesan was a pale representation of the real thing.

In one of my more creative moments, I looked into the refrigerator only to discover I was out of cheddar cheese. But I had parmesan. Eureka. I caught sight of the pecans I had in the fridge, and went, Hmm. Everyone always knows that's the sound of inspiration in the kitchen. I toasted those pecans right up and blended in parmesan instead of cheddar and created a new recipe. These babies are delicious. I've even served them as appetizers (making them into nugget-sized bites). The flavors may be a blend of Italian and Southern, but that's the great thing about cooking. There is always new magic to discover.

   4 tablespoons butter

   1½ cups flour

   1½ teaspoons baking powder

   ½ teaspoon salt

   2 eggs

   ¾ cup milk

   1 cup grated parmesan cheese

   ½ cup roasted pecans

My fast trick for roasting nuts is to simply chop them and then add them to a pan on the stove with a little melted butter, stirring constantly on medium heat until they are brown. When I'm making biscuits, I'm usually just ready to get them done with no prep. I put the nuts on a plate to cool in the refrigerator. If I need to grate parmesan, here's when I do it; otherwise, I simply use pre-grated (and yes, I do buy it sometimes because it's easy). Then I turn to making the dough.

Cut the butter into the flour, salt, and baking powder until the mixture is crumbly. Then add in the beaten eggs and milk and stir until incorporated. Fold in the grated parmesan and pecans. Roll the dough out to about one inch thickness and cut them into your desired shape. Lay the biscuits out a few inches apart on a greased cookie sheet. Bake at 400 degrees for 15-20 minutes.

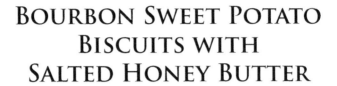

BOURBON SWEET POTATO BISCUITS WITH SALTED HONEY BUTTER

One of my favorite things to make in the fall and winter are my bourbon sweet mashed potatoes—a recipe I shared in Country Heaven Cookbook. When I have mashed sweet potatoes around, I usually get to thinking it would be super easy to make biscuits, especially if I have leftovers. They are already smooth and flavored with delicious additions like bourbon, cinnamon, clove, and honey.

I usually keep the sweet potatoes on low heat on the stove in the meantime. The other way I make mashed sweet potatoes is to pop one in the microwave until it's cooked, but this is my less favorite way. While these treats involve a little more prep than the others, they are pure delight to your loved ones around the table and well worth the effort.

Biscuits

4 tablespoons butter

1½ cups flour

1½ teaspoons baking powder

½ teaspoon salt

2 eggs

1 cup milk, as needed

¾ cup mashed sweet potatoes

Measure the amount of mashed sweet potatoes and combine it with the milk to cool it down. Again, you don't want your ingredients so warm they melt the butter in your dough upon contact. If the mixture doesn't cool down enough, I simply pop it into the freezer for a few minutes to cool. Prepare the dough by cutting the butter into the dry ingredients until the mixture is crumbly. Then beat the eggs and add them to the mashed sweet potato mixture (if you didn't add the milk to cool the sweet potatoes, simply add it to the bowl with the eggs). Here's an important point. Every mashed sweet potato I make varies in the moisture it has, so I sometimes have to add a little more milk or flour depending on the consistency of the dough. Just trust yourself. The dough should be a little sticky but not runny like batter.

Mix until incorporated and then roll out on a floured surface. When you have the dough rolled out to about an inch think, cut them into your favorite shape (did we talk about triangles yet?) and place them on a greased cookie sheet. Bake at 400 degrees for 15-20 minutes until golden brown.

Salted Honey Butter

> 8 tablespoons butter
>
> 1 teaspoon salt
>
> 2 tablespoons honey

Because these biscuits are already uniquely flavored, I decided one day to whip up a special Southern-inspired spread I called my Salted

Honey Butter. You can serve this with other breads, but this is a perfect pairing to these biscuits in particular.

Whip the butter, salt, and honey with a fork. The mixture will shape right up, trust me. I recommend tasting it to make sure it's sweet or salty enough for your palate. Depending on the honey I use (Tupelo is sweeter than orange blossom, for example), I might need to add a little more. Just mind the salt. It's harder to make something less salty.

Muffins

*H*er mom gave a belly laugh. *"All right, missy. Time to open your present."*

"You didn't have to get me anything, Mom," she said, pulling it onto her lap.

"Mother's prerogative," she said, patting Grace's leg.

"Ah, Mom," Grace said when she pulled out the small copper pot she recognized from her childhood. "This was Grandma's saucepan!" Grandma had splurged on the pan on a long-ago visit to Chicago, and for a time, she'd been the only woman in all of Deadwood to own one. It was a treasured family possession that had been passed down to Grace's mom ten years ago, upon Grandma's death.

"I don't use it much anymore," her mom said, tracing the wooden handle. "I thought you might like it. Maybe you can give it to Ella one day if she takes to cooking like you and I did."

Grace liked to think about all of the women in the family being connected by her grandma's special copper saucepan. They leaned closer to hug one another again.

~ Excerpt from Ava's The Gate to Everything

HOME *Baked* HAPPINESS

As a kid, muffins were bite-sized treats I could easily run outside with to continue playing before my mom called me inside for dinner. Of course this all depended on us having leftover muffins from breakfast, which didn't always happen with six kids, no surprise.

Some of my first memories of helping my grandma or mom in the kitchen were fitting the muffin tins with cupcake liners so the batter could be dropped in.

When I started working in my old profession of rebuilding warzones, I began to make nutrition-packed muffins I could either bring to the office or overseas when I traveled. I became known for my muffins and my creativity in combining various fruits, nuts, and grains. These muffins were all the more magical for the buttermilk I'd add.

Even now my mouth waters when I pick up a warm muffin dotted with a pad of butter. It feels like home to me, and it's a home I can easily carry with me to whatever part of the world I found myself in.

APPLESAUCE MUFFINS

These particular muffins were a favorite treat growing up on Saturday mornings while we were watching cartoons. There is nothing happier than the smell of apples, cinnamon, and bread baking in the oven, and this recipe involves all three. The melted butter topping with sugar and spices is especially decadent.

Muffins

2 cups flour

½ cup sugar

4 teaspoons baking powder

½ teaspoon salt

½ teaspoon cinnamon

¼ teaspoon nutmeg

1½ cups applesauce

4 tablespoons butter

1 egg

Melt the butter. Mix together the dry ingredients and then add the butter and applesauce. Stir. Beat the egg and add this as well, stirring until incorporated. Drop the batter into muffin tins. Bake at 400 degrees for 15-20 minutes; depending on the size of your muffin tins.

Topping

    3 tablespoons sugar

    ¼ teaspoon cinnamon

    ¼ teaspoon nutmeg

    4 tablespoons melted butter

When the muffins have cooled a touch, dress them with the topping. As a kid, I liked to dunk my muffin into the bowl containing the topping, but you can spoon it onto the top like a "civilized" person if you want. Either way, you're going to be smiling once this muffins hits your mouth.

BLUEBERRY MUFFINS

A common muffin in the household I grew up in involved fresh blueberries, which were always a treat. The blueberries would turn our lips and tongues blue, which would make us laugh like only kids can. Today I still love the sheer simplicity of this muffin, and yes, I find myself smiling when my lips and tongue turn blue. Being a kid at heart is a key to lifelong happiness.

>   8 tablespoons butter
>
>   1 cup sugar
>
>   2 eggs
>
>   1 teaspoon vanilla extract
>
>   2 teaspoons baking powder
>
>   ½ teaspoon salt
>
>   2 cups flour
>
>   ½ cup buttermilk
>
>   2 cups fresh blueberries

Cream together the butter and sugar. Add the eggs and vanilla and mix until incorporated. When the mixture is yellow and fluffy, add the flour, baking powder, and salt along with the buttermilk. Stir until everything is incorporated. Fold in the blueberries, being careful not to bruise the fruit. Drop the batter into muffin tins. Bake at 375 degrees for 25-30 minutes.

HONEY PUMPKIN SPICE MUFFINS

There's something magical about pumpkin muffins when they carry a hint of spice. When the weather turns cold, these come a calling. And I always answer...

3 eggs

8 tablespoons butter

2 cups flour

1 teaspoon baking soda

2 tablespoons baking powder

½ teaspoon salt

2 teaspoons cinnamon

1 teaspoon nutmeg

½ teaspoon cloves

1 cup buttermilk

2 cups canned pumpkin

1 cup honey

1 cup toasted pecans

Beat the eggs and then add in the dry ingredients of flour, soda, baking powder, salt, and spices. Melt the butter. Add the butter, the buttermilk, pumpkin, and honey to your batter and mix until incorporated. Chop your pecans and fold them in. Drop the batter into muffin tins. Bake at 350 degrees for 25-30 minutes.

GINGERBREAD MUFFINS

The magic of the holidays in a muffin... They always make me feel right at home. I grew up loving gingerbread cookies, but I wanted something besides a cookie to enjoy that had the same flavor. These muffins are a wonderful treat on cold mornings with a strong cup of coffee or tea. Top them with butter or honey, and you're going to close your eyes in delight for sure.

> 3 eggs
> ½ cup honey
> ½ cup molasses
> 1 teaspoon vanilla extract
> 2 cups flour
> 1 teaspoon baking soda
> 2 tablespoons baking powder
> 1 teaspoon salt
> 3 teaspoons cinnamon
> 2 teaspoons nutmeg
> 1 teaspoon cloves
> 2 tablespoons fresh ground ginger
> 8 tablespoons butter
> ¾ cup buttermilk

Beat the eggs and then add in the honey, molasses, and vanilla. Stir. Add in the dry ingredients of flour, soda, baking powder, salt, and spices. Melt the butter and add it and the buttermilk to your batter. Mix until incorporated. Drop the batter into muffin tins. Bake at 375 degrees for 25-30 minutes.

Scones

He dug into the basket for a stainless steel frozen container. "Open it."

When she did, her knees went weak. "You brought me their salted caramel and banana milkshake?"

His smile was lop-sided. "It is your favorite. And I stopped at the Rocky Mountain Chocolate Factory and bought you an English toffee apple."

Now she was deeply suspicious. "But you never approved of me eating that much sugar..." She bit off the words when we were together.

He barked out a laugh. "I was full of myself. I just want you to be happy, and little makes you happier than food."

Andy's words came back to her like a wave, powerful and impossible to fight. Blake did want her to be happy. Maybe it was time to stop fighting that quite so hard. "Thank you," she repeated, her throat clogged with emotion.

The smile turned into a besotted grin, the one she remembered from their courtship. He was embarrassed, but happy to have pleased her.

~ Excerpt from Ava's Bridge to a Better Life

My British fans will love knowing I have to give the Brits credit for giving me a love of scones...

It all started on my first visit to England when I was in college visiting a friend who lived in Suffolk. Her small country house was fragrant with sweet peas and always filled with buttery scones served with strawberry jam and something I'd never had before...clotted cream. It only took one sitting for us to become the best of friends.

When I returned from England, I had trouble finding clotted cream and making scones. For years, I experimented with different recipes until I had my aha moment. I needed buttermilk. After that, my scones were never dry and came out pitch perfect.

Now I've become known for my scones. When people come to visit, they even ask if I could make them for breakfast. I usually ask them what kind of flavors they are in the mood for, but if they don't have a clue, I just go with some old favorites I've developed.

LEMON BLUEBERRY SCONES

This particular scone has become a family favorite, and the inclusion of fresh lemon zest alongside the blueberries has really added to its decadent flavor. I make these in big batches to satisfy the crowd; if any are left they go into the freezer for future snacks when we're on the run or have a scone hankering.

16 tablespoons butter

5 cups flour

¾ teaspoon baking soda

1 tablespoon baking powder

1 teaspoon salt

¼ cup sugar

1¾ cups buttermilk

2½ cups fresh blueberries

2 tablespoons fresh lemon zest

Let the butter come to room temperature. Mix together the dry ingredients of flour, soda, baking powder, salt, and sugar. Cut the butter into the dry ingredients until crumbly and then add the buttermilk until the mixture is sticky. Fold in the blueberries and lemon zest.

Roll the dough out into a rectangle on a floured pastry cloth until it's about an inch thick. Scones are like biscuits in my opinion. The thicker they are, the less likely they are to overcook. Cut the scones into your desired shape. Triangles are the standard, but who made up that rule? I've done squares and circles when I'm feeling like I want something different. The shape doesn't affect the taste, after all.

Place the scones on a greased cookie sheet. Melt some butter and use a pastry brush to coat them; then sprinkle gourmet sugar on the tops of the individual scones. Bake at 400 degrees for about 20-25 minutes.

RHUBARB GINGER SCONES

Do you ever wish you had some new way to use the rhubarb in your garden? Well, that's how I felt one bright summer day. And then I thought. Scones! Fresh ginger seemed like the perfect complement, and this scone was born. A few people in the family weren't sure about this one when I made it the first time, but they promptly gobbled it up and have since asked for them again. It's a summer favorite.

16 tablespoons butter

5 cups flour

¾ teaspoon baking soda

1 tablespoon baking powder

1 teaspoon salt

¼ cup sugar

1¾ cups buttermilk

2½ cups freshly cut rhubarb

1 tablespoons fresh ginger

Cut the rhubarb stalks into small bite-sized pieces. Mince the ginger. Now you're ready to make the scones. Let the butter come to room temperature. Mix together the dry ingredients of flour, soda, baking powder, salt, and sugar. Cut the butter into the dry ingredients until crumbly and then add the buttermilk until the mixture is sticky. Fold in the rhubarb and ginger.

Roll the dough out into a rectangle on a floured

Home *Baked* Happiness

pastry cloth until it's about an inch thick. Cut the scones into your desired shape.

Place the scones on a greased cookie sheet. Melt some butter and use a pastry brush to coat them; then sprinkle gourmet sugar on the tops of the individual scones. Bake at 400 degrees for about 20-25 minutes.

Chocolate Chip Scones

Given how much I love scones, are you really surprised I have a scone featuring chocolate? That's right. Sometimes, you just want to have chocolate in your scones. Serve this with a dessert tea that has carob in it, and you'll be in heaven.

  16 tablespoons butter

  5 cups flour

  ¾ teaspoon baking soda

  1 tablespoon baking powder

  1 teaspoon salt

  ¼ cup sugar

  1¾ cups buttermilk

  2½ cups chocolate chips

Let the butter come to room temperature. Mix together the dry ingredients of flour, soda, baking powder, salt, and sugar. Cut the butter into the dry ingredients until crumbly and then add the buttermilk until the mixture is sticky. Add in the chocolate chips and stir until incorporated.

Roll the dough out into a rectangle on a floured pastry cloth until it's about an inch thick. Cut the scones into your desired shape.

Place the scones on a greased cookie sheet. Melt some butter and use a pastry brush to coat them; then sprinkle gourmet sugar on the tops of the individual scones. Bake at 400 degrees for about 20-25 minutes.

CHERRY VANILLA SCONES

I'm not sure what it is about dried cherries that gets me so excited, but I have to say, adding them to scones was a moment of sheer genius. Of course, pure vanilla extract seems to be the perfect pair to the cherries. I love having these with a cold dry champagne while I take a lovely walk through the garden and see what's blooming. The family especially likes these for a Sunday brunch.

16 tablespoons butter

5 cups flour

¾ teaspoon baking soda

1 tablespoon baking powder

1 teaspoon salt

¼ cup sugar

1¾ cups buttermilk

1 teaspoon pure vanilla extract

2 cups dried tart cherries

Let the butter come to room temperature. Mix together the dry ingredients of flour, soda, baking powder, salt, and sugar. Cut the butter into the dry ingredients until crumbly and then add the buttermilk and vanilla until the mixture is sticky. Add in the dried cherries and stir until incorporated.

Roll the dough out into a rectangle on a floured pastry cloth until it's about an inch thick. Cut the scones into your desired shape.

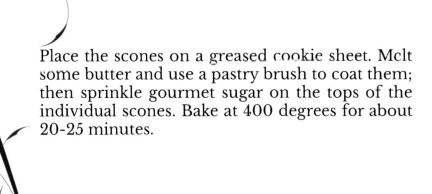

Place the scones on a greased cookie sheet. Mclt some butter and use a pastry brush to coat them; then sprinkle gourmet sugar on the tops of the individual scones. Bake at 400 degrees for about 20-25 minutes.

Cakes

"*Cooking will be healing for you,*" *Helga said when he removed his hand from the meat.*

"*What did you say?*" *he asked, still coming out of his childhood reverie. He wiped his hands off with the wet cloth she'd brought him.*

"*Food makes people happy,*" *she said, her full face transformed by a rare smile. "Happy people heal faster.*"

Chase knew medical professionals talked about such things, but it was hard to imagine it in regards to him.

"*Are you trying not to laugh?*" *she asked, ever perceptive. "Maybe you should. It might make you happy.*"

~ Excerpt from Ava's Home Sweet Love

Cakes captured my imagination at an early age. My mom was a master cake baker, and for our birthdays she would make cakes into animals or dolls or other shapes. Instead of paint, she used frosting to finish off her masterpieces. I realize now she was teaching me how baking could be an art form.

I love making cakes. Somehow people don't expect you to serve them cake or to bring it to their house for dessert. There's something so old-fashioned, so homey about cakes. And the sky's the limit on its structure. You can make it round or horizontal, tiered or layered. And the frosting choices...

At one point, I baked cakes for people's birthdays or special events as a way of making some extra cash for college. I'd invent grand masterpieces myself, taking a simple family chocolate cake and cutting it in half and spreading raspberries and toasted pine nuts in the middle and then covering it with a decadent chocolate ganache.

Now I make cakes when I feel the urge. Sometimes it's late at night after someone has had a "bad" day and needs some cheering up. Few things can turn a rainy day into a party like cake. Or make you feel so at home.

ANGEL FOOD CAKE

Whoever named this cake knew what they were talking about because it's like eating sugar-coated clouds. Growing up, this cake was served often and with lots of love—plus decadent sides like strawberries and whipped cream. But we also figured out how to make a Chocolate Angel Food cake too, continuing with the chocolate theme.

Meringue

> 1½ cups egg whites
>
> 1½ teaspoons cream of tartar
>
> 1½ teaspoons vanilla
>
> ¼ teaspoon salt
>
> 1⅓ cups sugar

Cake

> 1¼ cups cake flour
>
> ½ cup sugar

Sift the dry ingredients for the cake —the flour and sugar—a couple of times. Now it's time to make the meringue. In large bowl, combine egg whites (room temperature is best), cream of tartar, vanilla, and salt. Beat until soft peaks form. Add the sugar in increments and keep beating. When stiff peaks form, cut with the flat side of a knife to test the firmness of the meringue. The knife should make a clear path, rather like parting the Red Sea. Fold in the sifted cake ingredients gently. To ensure there are no air bubbles, make more cuts with a knife in the cake batter in diagonal passes.

Place the batter in an ungreased angel food cake pan. Bake at 375 degrees for 35 minutes until golden brown on top. When the cake has finished baking, carefully turn the cake down by arranging it over a sturdy bottle and let rest. The cake will not fall out, so don't worry. When cooled, turn right-side up, cut the cake out of the pan, and arrange it on a plate. It's time to eat!

Note: For a Chocolate Angel Food Cake, add 2 tablespoons cocoa powder to the cake ingredients.

Yellow Cake

This yellow cake is a family staple, and when I grew up, new members of the family have gravitated to it because they simply love yellow cake! I'm always going to prefer a chocolate cake, but since I love them, we bake this one and compromise on the frosting. Chocolate buttercream icing is one of my favorites and goes beautifully with this cake.

10 tablespoons butter

1¾ cups sugar

2 eggs

1½ teaspoons vanilla

3 cups cake flour

2½ teaspoons baking powder

1 teaspoon salt

1¼ cups milk

Cream together the butter and sugar; then add the eggs and vanilla. Add the remaining ingredients and mix until smooth. Pour the batter into two 9-inch round pans. Bake at 350 degrees for 30-35 minutes.

GERMAN CHOCOLATE CAKE

Growing up, I was at the tail end of the birthday train. By the time we got around to mine, I was tired of our regular white cake. One summer I asked for a different cake, and I choose German Chocolate. I didn't know about the magic of buttermilk then, but my grandma must have known. I still remember my grandma making the frosting on the stove; I often spent my birthday there since we were out of school for the summer. This cake always takes me back to those magical days where we celebrated my coming into the world as a family—a happy occasion.

    8 ounces chocolate
    ½ cup boiling water
    8 tablespoons butter
    1¼ cups sugar
    4 egg yolks
    1 teaspoon vanilla
    2½ cups cake flour
    1 teaspoon baking soda
    ½ teaspoon salt
    1 cup buttermilk
    4 egg whites

Chop the chocolate and melt it in the boiling water. Cool. Sift together the flour, soda, and salt. Cream the butter and the sugar. Mix in the egg yolks and vanilla. Now stir in the cool chocolate mixture until incorporated. Add the dry ingredients and buttermilk, mixing thoroughly. Fold in the egg whites. Pour the batter into a cake pan; circle, square, or rectangle—your choice. Bake at 350 degrees for 25-30 minutes until you can insert a toothpick into the cake and it comes out clean. The cooking time may be a little more or less depending on the shape and size of your pan fyi. Cool the cake.

Frosting

> 1 cup cream
>
> 1 cup sugar
>
> 1 teaspoon vanilla
>
> 3 egg yolks
>
> 8 tablespoons butter
>
> 1⅓ cups shredded coconut
>
> 1 cup pecans, chopped

Mix the cream, sugar, vanilla, and egg yolks in a sauce pan until incorporated. Put on medium heat on the stove and cook until slightly bubbling. The mixture should thicken a touch. Add in the butter and stir. Now add the coconut and pecan and mix thoroughly. When the frosting is cooled, frost the cake.

BUTTERMILK CHOCOLATE CAKE

As I said, I'm a buttermilk aficionado when it comes to baking, and this cake fits me to a tee with the addition of chocolate—my other favorite. For a time after my best friend and neighbor died of cancer, I'd make this cake as a way of celebrating her life in the midst of tremendous grief. Julia loved cake, and we often ate one I'd baked next door with hibiscus tea. I knew she'd love this kind of tribute. Plus it's one of the best cakes I've ever eaten.

12 tablespoons butter

1 cup sugar

2 eggs

1 teaspoon vanilla

1 ¾ cups flour

¾ cup cocoa powder

2 teaspoons baking soda

1 teaspoon baking powder

1 teaspoon salt

1 cup buttermilk

1 cup hot coffee

Before you make the batter, prepare your hot coffee. For baking purposes, I like to use some nice instant espresso powder and mix it with hot water, but you can brew a pot of coffee to drink while making this recipe. When finished, cream together the butter and sugar. Then add the eggs and vanilla and beat until light and fluffy. Now add in the dry ingredients of flour, cocoa, soda, baking powder, and salt. Mix thoroughly while adding the buttermilk.

The batter will be smooth. Time to add the hot coffee. The batter will change color and texture, but don't worry. It's supposed to. Pour into two 9-inch round pans. Bake at 350 degrees for 30-35 minutes. When the cake is finished, remove from the oven and run a knife along the sides to loosen the cake. Then flip it onto wax paper to cool.

Like I said, you can top this with whipped cream or a frosting of your choice. Both a white and chocolate frosting works great, but why not a hazelnut chocolate or chocolate raspberry frosting? I just go with wherever the inspiration takes me.

Pies

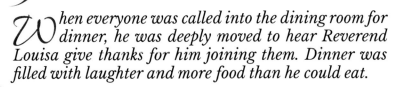

hen everyone was called into the dining room for dinner, he was deeply moved to hear Reverend Louisa give thanks for him joining them. Dinner was filled with laughter and more food than he could eat.

He'd thought he'd have to fight the urge to check work emails, but he didn't once have the inclination. Conversation flowed, and Amelia Ann left him to have some girl chat with the McGuiness sisters.

Seated alone on the couch, he took a moment to study the room. There were clusters of people everywhere, and all of them were either laughing or touching each other out of the sheer joy of being together.

He was a part of this now, and he bowed his head for a moment.

~ Excerpt from Ava's Fireflies And Magnolias

Few things make me feel at home like pies. I grew up with pies baking in the oven every Sunday. Cherry and apple were favorites growing up, but we also enjoyed a magical frozen pie with whipped cream and strawberries. During the summer months, this one was especially cooling to our warm bodies after running around outside and climbing trees.

As I grew older, baking pies was less convenient since I was single. But then I discovered small pie dishes... Suddenly I could make an apple pie just for me—a pure treat. This transformed my pie baking.

Now we don't often bring out the individual pie plates. We goggle up whole pies and savor the leftovers the next day.

Pies continues to bring a smile to my face, and when I make them, I'm cooking up home baked happiness for sure.

FAMILY PIE CRUST

I continue to experiment with what makes the crispiest and flakiest crust along with my sister, who has gotten her baking shoes on. I think we've struck upon the secret. It's the combination of both butter and Crisco in equal measure. Each brings different properties to the mix, and every time it's magic.

> 2 cups flour
> ½ teaspoon salt
> ½ cup butter
> ½ cup Crisco
> ¼ cup cold water

Cut the butter and Crisco into the dry ingredients until incorporated (not too much, but just until it comes together). Add the cold water; we put ¼ cup water in a measuring cup and add ice to it. Mix until everything comes together. Then roll out onto a floured surface into a circle. Lay the crust into the pie plate and flute the edges by pinching the dough on the top and sides between your two index fingers. Dot the pie crust with a fork across the bottom before baking to prevent air holes. This recipes makes two pie halves (either a top and a bottom or two bottoms depending on the pie you're making).

TOFFEE-CRUSTED APPLE PIE

Growing up we didn't have the range of apple varieties we have now. In a pinch, I use Granny Smith because I like a tart pie, but you can use a combination of apple types for more balance. I've also used Fuji and Pink Lady with great success. Experiment. See what you like. That's my favorite part of cooking.

Prepare 1 crust for the bottom of the pie.

Apple Mixture

6-7 cups thinly sliced apples

¾ cup sugar

2 tablespoons flour

¾ teaspoon ground cinnamon

1 tablespoon lemon juice

Mix all the ingredients in a bowl until flour is incorporated, and the mixture is thickened. Place in an uncooked crust.

Toffee Topping

1 cup flour

8 tablespoons butter

½ cup sugar

Mix the ingredients with a pastry wheel or a fork

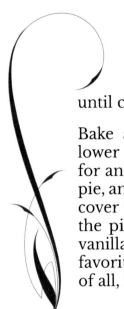

until crumbly and place on the top of the apples.

Bake at 425 degrees for 15 minutes, and then lower the temperature to 350 degrees and bake for another 35-40 minutes. Check the top of the pie, and if it's browning too much toward the end, cover the top with aluminum foil. You will know the pie is done when it bubbles. I serve it with vanilla ice cream or sea salt caramel, one of my favorites. See what works best for you, but most of all, have fun!

FAMILY APPLE TART

Our family has a strong love of all things French, especially when it comes to pastries. I remember the day I had my first tart. I was in Lyon after my study abroad had ended, and I sighted a strawberry tart on a local pastry cart. At that time, I didn't know what a food capital Lyon is. All I knew is that I had to have whatever that strawberry thing was shining under the sunny blue sky. I pretty much polished it off, and a few more over the next couple days.

Now my sister and I often make an apple tart to please the masses; we always have apples in the refrigerator. I recently realized that tarts are the French version of pies, although my French friends might argue with me. Regardless, these are a wonderful addition to anyone's baking, and my sister and I have mastered the crust in the family (okay, mostly her—haha). Give it a shot and prepare to be wowed.

Tart Crust

8 tablespoons butter
1 cup flour
½ teaspoon salt
1 tablespoon sugar
¼ cup cold water

Cut the butter into the dry ingredients of flour, salt, and sugar until crumbly. Add the cold water. Mix until everything comes together. Then

roll out onto a floured surface into a circle. Lay the crust into a tart pan and flute the edges by pinching the dough on the top and sides between your two index fingers.

Now comes our secret. Combine 1 tablespoon of both flour and sugar and sprinkle onto the bottom of the crust. Seriously, it's that easy.

Fork the bottom of the tart.

Filling

> 3-4 apples, thinly sliced
>
> 1 tablespoon sugar
>
> 2 tablespoons butter

For the filling, arrange the apple slices until the bottom is full. Sprinkle the sugar on top (add more if you want it sweeter depending on your apples). Melt the butter and drizzle it over the mixture. Chill the uncooked tart for 10 minutes and then bake at 400 degrees for 40-50 minutes. Make sure to put a lipped cookie sheet under your tart pan while cooking.

MILE HIGH STRAWBERRY PIE

Interestingly this pie goes back to my baby shower if you can believe it. I kinda like thinking I was celebrated with something so scrumptious. It was like they already knew I was a food lover, even though I was in the womb. This recipe was our summer treat growing up when the days were hot and fresh, plump strawberries were easily available in the market. The sweet, airiness of the pie is beautifully contrasted by the salty sweet crust. You're gonna love this one...

Crust

> 1⅓ cups flour
>
> 2 tablespoons milk
>
> 1½ tablespoons sugar
>
> ½ cup oil
>
> 1 teaspoon salt

Put the flour, sugar and salt in a 9 by 13 inch pan. Whip the milk and oil together with a fork in a separate bowl. Pour it on top of the dry mixture in the pan. Mix with a fork and press the crust evenly onto the bottom of the pan and the sides. Bake at 425 degrees for about 10-12 minutes until brown. Cool.

Filling

2 egg whites

1 tablespoon lemon juice

1 10 ounce package frozen strawberries (thawed) or 1 quart fresh strawberries mashed

2 cups whipped cream

1 cup sugar

Beat egg whites until foamy. Add strawberries, sugar, and lemon juice. Turn up mixer to high and beat for 15-20 minutes. Fold in the whipped cream and spread the mixture into your pan. Freeze thoroughly.

Cookies

For the next two hours, laughter was the main sound in the kitchen. Tory orchestrated the entire production, helping them roll dough, cut cookies, and then peel them off the flour-dusted counter and onto a cookie sheet. Coloring the frosting added another piece of fun with Annabelle trying to achieve the perfect shade of pink.

Rory finally relaxed and was swept away. He didn't get the giggles like Annabelle, who was clearly on a sugar high, but he smiled more and acted less guarded. Rye couldn't hold back a grin as the boy settled closer to him, announcing that the two of them were making manly cookies with manly icing.

When Tammy and Mama walked into the kitchen, cookies covered every surface. Rye was helping Rory finish decorating his soldier while Amelia Ann and Tory were adding the last silver ball to one of Annabelle's princess cookies.

~ Excerpt from Ava's Country Heaven

We didn't have a cookie jar growing up. We had an old plastic ice cream bucket, which often rested on the kitchen counter. We always had cookies growing up, and that's something I'm grateful to my mom for. She never denied up sweets. She knew the power of balance. We always ate well, even though it wasn't like we consciously thought about it. If you asked anyone in our family about how we ate, they'd simply shrug and respond, "home cooked meals." And that was true...

Around the holidays, we had more cookie varieties than you could shake a stick at. I remember strategically arranging the portions on my plate for dinner so I would have room for the goodies in more plastic ice cream buckets stored on the very cold enclosed front porch.

Cookies meant love, and when I was working in my old career I'd bake my famous chocolate chip cookies for my colleagues as a thank you for their hard work on a project. My chocolate chip cookies ended up receiving international fame, the story of which I tell with the recipe, so keep reading.

Chocolate Chip Cookies

If there is one signature baking item I'm known for, it's my chocolate chip cookies. People have asked me to make them in lieu of birthday cakes even. True story...in my former career of working in developing countries, I used to bring my cookies as gifts for business colleagues to show appreciation. There's a long tradition of giving sweets a gifts in many of the cultures I worked in. In Egypt, my cookies got some fame, and I had investors approach me about making me the Mrs. Fields of Egypt, something I just didn't feel was my path. For me, these cookies are the embodiment of home-baked happiness.

16 tablespoons butter

¾ cup sugar

¾ brown sugar

1 teaspoon vanilla

2 eggs

2¾ cups flour

1 teaspoon salt

1 teaspoon baking soda

2 cups chocolate chips

1 cup walnuts

The trick I've found to making blue-ribbon cookies is to chill the dough and then drop them into balls about two to three inches in diameter. This allows for the cookies to stay soft on the inside, something that's often problematic with smaller cookies. Get ready for these treats to transform your day. When I'm pressed for time, I pop the dough into the freezer until they are chilled and then go from there. I mean, how many of us think about making cookies a day early? I know I don't. I bake to my schedule and figure out ways to ensure I'm adhering to technique while I'm at it.

Cream the butter and white and brown sugar. Add the eggs and vanilla and beat until incorporated. Now add in the flour, salt, and soda, stirring thoroughly. Chop the walnuts and fold them into the batter with the chocolate chips. Cool the dough. Drop two to three inch balls of dough on a cookie sheet, ensuring space to expand. Bake these cookies at 375 degrees, first for five minutes on the bottom rack and then finishing them for another 5 minutes on the top rack.

SALTED OATMEAL COOKIES

When it comes to desserts, I appreciate the salty sweet variety. Someone gave me a salted oatmeal cookie once, and I was thunder struck. I'd grown up with the traditional oatmeal raisin. The addition of salt on the top was a fabulous idea. I decided to play with our traditional recipe to recreate the cookie I'd eaten. While you can add raisins to these cookies, I often bake them without them. They are so well balanced and satisfying. The trick is to find a good salt to dot them with, and thankfully gourmet salts are widely available now.

12 tablespoons butter

1 cup brown sugar

½ cup white sugar

2 eggs

1 teaspoon vanilla

1¾ cups flour

1 teaspoon salt

1 teaspoon baking powder

¼ teaspoon baking soda

½ teaspoon cinnamon

2 cups old-fashioned oats

¼ cup raisins (optional)

Cream together the two kinds of sugar with the butter and then add the eggs and vanilla, mixing thoroughly. Stir in the flour, salt, baking powder, soda, and cinnamon until incorporated. Fold in the rolled oats and raisins (these cookies are just as delicious without them fyi). Cool the dough and then form into two to three inch balls on a cookie sheet. Sprinkle a rough-ground salt (kosher, Celtic, fleur de sel, etc.) over the tops of the cookie balls. Bake at 375 degrees for 14-16 minutes until golden brown, switching between the bottom and top racks in the oven for smoother cooking.

LINCOLN LOGS

If I had to pick one of my favorite holiday cookies, this would be it. Perhaps it's because they are covered in chocolate and have a little salty sweet medley going on in the middle... They take a little more work than most cookies even though they aren't cooked, but they are well worth the effort, especially around the holidays.

Cookies

    8 tablespoons butter

    1 cup chunky peanut butter

    2 cups powdered sugar

    2 cups Rice Krispies

    1 cup shredded coconut

    ½ cup walnuts, chopped

Chocolate

    12 ounces chocolate chips

    1 ounce paraffin

Cream the butter and the powdered sugar together until incorporated. Stir in the peanut butter and then fold in the Rice Krispies, coconut, and the chopped walnuts. Form the cookies into small log shapes of about three inches. Place on a baking rack with a lipped cookie sheet under them. Make your chocolate mixture by melting the chocolate chips with the paraffin on the stove on low heat.

When the chocolate is cool, but still resembling a sauce, pour over the cookies. After the cookies have set, remove the excess chocolate from the lipped cookie sheet and add back to the mixture. Now turn the cookies over and cover them on this side with the chocolate. Of course you can dip them each, but that takes longer in my opinion, and you still needed to touch up your fingerprints or tong marks. When the chocolate is set, pop one of these babies into your mouth and wait for the fireworks.

GINGER MOLASSES COOKIES

While chocolate chip is one of my favorites, a chewy ginger molasses cookie will also transport my taste buds to thoughts of home and happiness. I remember having these cookies when I was a kid, and the gingerbread-like flavor along with the chewiness was intoxicating. Now I love to have it with a cappuccino or a strong cup of tea.

12 tablespoons butter

1½ cups sugar

2 eggs

1 teaspoon vanilla

½ cup molasses

4 cups flour

2 teaspoons salt

2 teaspoons baking soda

1 tablespoon baking powder

2 teaspoons ground cinnamon

2 teaspoons ginger

1 teaspoon ground cloves

1 teaspoon nutmeg

Special sugar for dusting

Cream together the butter and sugar and then add in the eggs and vanilla. When light and fluffy, add in the molasses and then the rest of the dry ingredients and the spices, careful not to over mix. For the ginger, I sometimes use fresh, finely chopping it until it resembles a paste. Cool the dough and then form into two to three inch balls, placing them on a cookie sheet a few inches apart. Sprinkle the tops of the cookies with a gourmet sugar like demerara. Bake at 350 degrees for about 14-16 minutes, switching from the bottom to the top rack in the oven.

I hope you enjoyed baking with me and sharing stories. I wish you much home baked happiness in your life. I couldn't think of better last words for this cookbook than these...

When I first set out on my goddess transformation, I didn't fully know what made me happy. I hadn't truly felt happy since I was a child, and most of the things I spent my time on where on the "should do" or "shouldn't do" list. I had all these rules I'd taken on about needing to be responsible, serious, adult. None of it connected me to a sense of enchantment, except my love of food (and I mean cooking it and eating it) and stories. I loved movies; I loved reading books; and I loved writing my own stories. I was quite simply enchanted.

This list turned out to be more than just things to do. I realized my happiness also got boosted when I simply gave myself what I needed. By giving to myself, I ended up loving and appreciating all that made me up. That is its own kind of enchantment. I was celebrating the enchanting goddess I am.

~ Excerpt from Ava's Goddesses Are Happy

To enjoy Ava's other books touching on home baked happiness, here's a helpful list to tempt your reading taste buds. All are stand-alone books to cuddle up with when you're looking for that perfect inspiring, comfort read.

Country Heaven

Country Heaven Cookbook

Fireflies and Magnolias

French Roast

The Perfect Ingredient

The Bridge to A Better Life

Home Sweet Love

The Gate to Everything

Goddesses Eat

Goddesses Are Happy

All of Ava's books can be found on her website:

www.avamiles.com

About Ava

Former chef and International Bestselling Author Ava Miles joined the ranks of beloved storytellers with her powerful messages of healing, mystery, and magic. Millions of readers have discovered her fiction and nonfiction books, praised by *USA TODAY* and *Publisher's Weekly*. *Women's World Magazine* has selected a few of her novels for their book clubs while Southwest Airlines featured the #1 National Bestseller *NORA ROBERTS LAND* (the name used with Ms. Roberts' blessing) in its in-flight entertainment. Ava's books have been chosen as Best Books of the Year and Top Editor's Picks and are translated into multiple languages.

Ava calls herself a divine rockstar, something she believes everyone is deep down. She's a unique expression of love and joy in the world with her own special gifts: writing stories with uplifting messages, being an intuitive healer, inspiring others to uncover their authentic selves and their highest path in the world; and creating artistic masterpieces like pottery and sculptures. And then there's the cooking... She used to be a chef and rocks food big time.

A global awakener at the core, Ava has dedicated her life to uplifting everyone on the planet. In her former career rebuilding war zones, she worked in places like Lebanon, Colombia, Pakistan, West Bank/Gaza, and Congo to foster peaceful communities. Now she's sharing her stories of love, forgiveness, and empowerment around the world—pretty much still changing lives.

Join Ava in letting your brilliance shine through. For more information, visit www.avamiles.com.

Made in the USA
Coppell, TX
01 June 2020